COLUMBUS DAY

by Robin Nelson

first step nonfiction

Lerner Publications Company · Minneapolis

JOSEPH CERVETTO, JR.
CHRISTOPHER COLUMBUS

COLUMBUS

We **celebrate** Columbus Day every year.

2009 October

SUNDAY	MONDAY	TUESDAY	WEDNESDAY	THURSDAY	FRIDAY	SATURDAY
				1	2	3
4	5	6	7	8	9	10
11	12 Columbus Day	13	14	15	16	17
18	19	20	21	22	23	24
25	26	27	28	29	30	31

This holiday is on the second Monday in October.

We remember the day
Columbus came to the
Americas.

Christopher Columbus was an **explorer**.

He sailed across an ocean.

After sailing for a long time,
he saw land.

He started in Europe.

He thought he had gone
around the world and
landed in Asia.

North America

West Indies

South America

But this was land he did not know was there.

He found **native people** in
this new land.

Over the years, more people
went to this new land.

Many years later, people
celebrated Columbus Day.

On this holiday, we learn
about Christopher Columbus.

We learn about the native
people he met.

We celebrate with **parades**.

We remember a man who explored the world.

Columbus Day Timeline

October 12, 1492
Christopher Columbus came to the Americas.

October 12, 1792
The first Columbus Day was celebrated 300 years after Columbus found America.

1905
Colorado was the first state to have an official Columbus Day.

1971
President Richard Nixon made Columbus Day the second Monday in October.

1937
President Franklin Roosevelt named October 12 Columbus Day.

Columbus Day Facts

 Christopher Columbus was not looking for a new world when he found land in 1492. He was searching for a shortcut from Spain to India.

 The land Columbus found was an island in the West Indies near Florida.

Columbus thought he was in India, so he called the native people Indians.

 The journey from Europe to America was over 3,000 miles.

Columbus's arrival was hard on native people. Some of his crew fought with them. Many native people died, and many were made into slaves.

 The Pledge of Allegiance was said for the first time at the Columbus Day celebration in 1892.

 There are many places named after Christopher Columbus, including Columbus, Ohio, and the country Colombia.

Glossary

 celebrate – to have a party or special activity to honor a special occasion

 explorer – a person who travels in search of something

 native people – people from that land

 parades – people marching and putting on a show

Index

The images in this book are used with the permission of: AP Photo/Paul Sakuma, pp. 2, 22 (1st from top); © Independent Picture Service, p. 3; © Stock Montage/SuperStock, p. 4; © SuperStock, Inc./SuperStock, pp. 5, 14, 22 (2nd from top); © North Wind Picture Archives, pp. 6, 15, 17; Everett Collection, p. 7; © Laura Westlund/Independent Picture Service, pp. 8–9, 10; © Image Asset Management Ltd./SuperStock, pp. 11, 22 (3rd from top); Mary Evans Picture Library/ Everett Collection, p. 12; Library of Congress (LC-DIG-ggbain-11301), p. 13; © Arnaldo Magnani/Getty Images, pp. 16, 22 (4th from top).
Cover: © Stock Montage/Hulton Archive/Getty Images.

Lerner Publications Company
A division of Lerner Publishing Group, Inc.
241 First Avenue North
Minneapolis, MN 55401 USA

For reading levels and more information, look up this title at www.lernerbooks.com.

Library of Congress Cataloging-in-Publication Data

Nelson, Robin, 1971–
    Columbus Day / by Robin Nelson.
        p.   cm. — (First step nonfiction. American holidays)
    Includes index.
    ISBN 978–0–7613–4928–0 (lib. bdg. : alk. paper)
    1. Columbus Day—Juvenile literature. 2. Columbus, Christopher—Juvenile literature.
    3. America—Discovery and exploration—Spanish—Juvenile literature. I. Title.
    E120.N456 2010
    394.264—dc22   2009010591

Manufactured in China
3 – SS – 1/1/14